Make Your Own
Dream Catcher

Jaclyn Crupi

hinkler

About this Book

This book contains everything you need to know to make a range of beautiful and eye-catching dream catchers.

To make dream catchers you will need:

- Hoops
- Coloured beads
- Brightly coloured feathers
- Coloured cords
- Coloured threads
- Charms
- Craft glue
- Scissors
- Needle
- Plain and lace ribbons

Contents

What Are Dreams?

Dreams are stories and images that our brains make while we are asleep. You might be surprised to learn that when you are sleeping your body is resting but your brain is very busy.

While You're Asleep

Your brain has lots of jobs to do while you are asleep. It needs to help you remember things by moving experiences to memory, help you sort out what's important and what's not, and tell you stories to help you make sense of things. Your brain is most active during REM (rapid eye movement) sleep and this is when the most vivid dreams are likely to occur. You can have up to six dreams every night!

Why Can't I Remember My Dreams?

Your brain is designed to help you hold on to information and store memories when you're awake and it usually does that well. It's not designed to help you hold on to information while you're asleep. This is why you often can't remember your dreams, or at least not all of your dreams. Scientists are not exactly sure why this is the case, but one theory is that dreams might be a distraction from paying attention to what's important during the day when you're awake. You're most likely to remember a dream if you wake up during a REM cycle.

What Are Dreams About?

Your dreams may feature people you know, but they may also include people you've never met and places you've never gone. They're usually about something you have strong feelings about. It might be what you're looking forward to or what you're nervous about. Your dreams are often based on things that are important to you.

Scary Dreams

Scientists don't know exactly why we have scary dreams, though they think it might be because our brains need to make sense of our fears. Dreams help us to process and understand the things that worry and scare us. They can help us to deal with difficult things we face in life. Scary dreams, or nightmares, are really just intense dreams.

Dream Meanings

Many people believe that dreams have hidden meanings, even dreams that seem to make no sense. Our brains are amazing. Did you know that more than 100,000 chemical reactions take place in your brain every second? Or that a piece of brain tissue the size of a grain of sand contains 100,000 neurons and 1 billion synapses, all communicating with each other? If you want to think about your dreams and what they mean for you, make sure you write them down when you wake in the morning.

What Are Dream Catchers?

Dream catchers are handmade objects made of thread that is woven onto hoops and decorated with feathers and beads. They originated in Native American tribes. They are designed to give peaceful dreams to their owners by trapping, or catching, any bad or unwanted dreams.

Shapes and Sizes

Dream catchers come in lots of different dimensions and there are no rules as to exactly how they need to be woven. In this book we'll give you lots of different design options and steps to follow for various-sized dream catchers, from a small and wearable necklace to a hula-hoop-sized option!

Catching Dreams

It is believed that the dream catcher, when hung over or near a bed, will catch dreams as they pass by. Good dreams know how to pass through the woven web of the dream catcher and will gently slide down the dangling, soft feathers and flow into your mind. Bad dreams don't know how to pass through the woven dream-catcher web and will get tangled and trapped. It's believed that the bad dreams then disappear when the sun rises.

The Gift of Sweet Dreams

Traditionally, dream catchers were given to newborn babies and to newly married couples. That tradition continues today and it is thought it's best to be given a homemade dream catcher rather than buying a ready-made one. So, once you have made yourself a dream catcher or two, you might like to make some for the special people in your life and give them as gifts.

Woven Wonders

The inner woven sections of dream catchers can be simple or they can be quite elaborate. They are the central parts of all dream catchers.

Mandala

The inner woven section of a dream catcher often contains a mandala. 'Mandala' means 'circle' in Sanskrit and refers to any circular pattern that represents the universe. When used within a dream catcher, the mandala is designed to bring our attention to how elaborately our lives are constructed. It's meant to make us consider the power we have to construct our lives and to rebuild them when we need to. It's a reminder that our thoughts are powerful and we have the ability to dream big and make our dreams come true.

Dream-Catcher Origins

Dream catchers originated in North America with the Ojibwe tribe, and over time the tradition of making them spread to neighbouring Native American tribes. The Ojibwe word for dream catcher is *asabikeshiinh* and means 'spider'. The tradition is thousands of years old.

Newborns

Legend says that the tradition of making dream catchers began with making them for newborns. Ojibwe women would make a dream catcher for each newborn baby to help ensure they had good dreams and also to entertain them when they woke. These dream catchers were made of willow and were not meant to last, eventually collapsing and signifying the end of the child's youth.

Spider Web

Traditionally, dream catchers were made to closely resemble spider webs. They often connect to the hoop at eight points, symbolising a spider's eight legs. There are many Native American legends about the Spider Woman (Asibikaashi) who cared for her children and the people of the land. It was thought that in case she couldn't look after all the children, women needed to make a web-like dream catcher for each new child.

Meanings

Each part of the traditional dream catcher has special meanings for Native Americans. The circle of the hoop signifies the circle of life and is linked to the sun and the moon. The web shape of the inner section signifies the Spider Woman's protective web, designed to allow good dreams through and to trap bad dreams. The feathers are thought of as sacred and they signify breath or air. The beads are thought to signify either the Spider Woman herself or the good dreams that could not pass through the web.

Dream Catchers Today

In modern times, the popularity of dream catchers has spread far and wide. The design and use of dream catchers has also changed. They are now often seen as decorative objects that can hang anywhere. Charms and other decorative elements have been added to the design.

Colour Meanings

Native Americans attributed meanings to certain colours and used them in face paints, tattoos, clothing and in times of war. These colours communicated messages to their tribe. Despite there being many Native American tribes, the significance of colours was often shared across long distances and with different people.

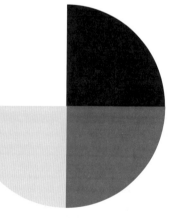

Face Paint

Face paint was used for celebrations and ceremonial traditions whereas war paint was used in times of battle with enemies. When used as face paint, as distinct from war paint, the following colours had these meanings. You might want to consider these meanings when choosing the colours for your dream catchers.

Black: Victory and success

Red: Faith, beauty and happiness

White: Sharing, purity and light

Yellow: Intellect and determination

Green: Nature, harmony and healing

Blue: Wisdom and intuition

Purple: Power, mystery and magic

The Medicine Wheel

Native Americans had a coloured circular medicine wheel, sometimes known as the sacred hoop. This wheel was used for health and healing. Each colour represented a part of the lifespan of a human.

White
represented death and intellectual life

Black
represented maturity and physical life

Yellow
represented growth and emotional life

Red
represented birth and spiritual life

Colours and Mood

Some people believe colours can affect your mood. If you're making a dream catcher for somebody, you could incorporate colours to help their mood; for example, you could use yellow (happiness) and blue (peace) if your friend is having a bad week.

Orange: Welcoming

Yellow: Happiness

Green: Harmony

Blue: Peace

Purple: Luxury

Black: Power

White: Simplicity

Brown: Friendliness

Colours and Dream Catchers

The colours you choose for your dream catchers will bring them to life. Feel free to experiment with interesting colour combinations. The colours of the threads, beads and feathers you choose will all come together to make the perfect dream catcher.

Getting Started

Before you can get started making your own dream catchers, there are some things you need to know. You should also ensure you have everything you need close at hand so making your dream catchers is fun and easy.

Materials

To make a dream catcher, you will need a hoop, coloured beads, feathers, coloured thread, coloured cord, a needle, glue, scissors and ribbons. You can buy these materials at most craft or fabric stores, or online.

The Hoop

No matter how you choose to design and decorate your dream catcher, you must have a frame. Metal, wooden or plastic hoops are all fine. The size of the hoop you use is up to you and determined by how large or small you want your dream catcher to be.

Cord and Thread

You can use cord, thread, fabric or wool to wrap the hoop. The inner woven section should be quite delicate and intricate, so a thinner thread is required.

First Things First

All dream catcher designs start the same way: by decorating the hoop. The most common way to do this is to wrap cord, thread, wool or fabric around the hoop. You can use a single-colour cord or thread for this or you can change the colour cord or thread as many times as you like. You can also use fabric to cover the hoop or, if you particularly like your hoop, you don't have to wrap it at all. You could even paint it! Metallic spray paint looks best, though you can use any paint that is appropriate for your hoop material.

Think it Through

It's best to think about the colours and look you want for your dream catcher before you start. Do you want to use neutral colours and keep it simple or do you want a bright design with lots of embellishments? Being clear in your mind about this before you start will make it easier.

Dream-Catcher Decoration

A hoop and woven thread are essentials for all dream catchers, but where they really take on a unique look is in the embellishments – feathers, charms, beads and ribbons! Adding these decorative elements will give your dream catchers your personal stamp and make them special.

Charms

Charms are a modern addition to dream catchers. They add something personal. Charms are mostly used in jewellery making, so adding them to dream catchers gives a contemporary twist. If you're making a dream catcher for a friend or family member, you can really personalise it by using charms that have the initials of that person on them.

Feathers

The idea that good dreams cascade down the dangling feathers is a key part of dream-catcher folklore, so it's important to think through what style of feathers you will use on each dream catcher you make. You can, of course, choose not to add feathers, but they are a key feature of the traditional dream catcher.

Beads

Beads add bursts of colour to the woven inner section of a dream catcher. Beads can be wooden or plastic and come in a huge range of colours. It's useful to separate your beads according to colour so you can easily select the ones you want for your design. You can add beads in a symmetrical way or you can add them randomly for dots of colour.

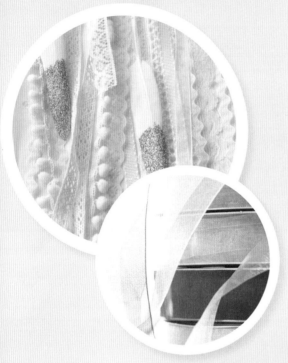

Ribbons

Use ribbons to suspend the dream catcher above your bed as well as to make it look extra dreamy! You can find them in the ribbon section of a fabric or craft store. To match the light, willowy look of dream catchers, we recommend lacy or gauze ribbons. Pom-pom ribbon looks great on more contemporary designs.

Bringing It All Together

All of these embellishments come together in your dream-catcher design. Don't feel like you have to use all of them in every dream catcher you make — sometimes less is more — but feel free to mix and match and use these decorations as you choose to make the dream catchers of your dreams!

Weaving Basics

Before you can get started designing your own dream catchers, you need to understand some weaving basics. The inner web of the dream catcher is the hardest part to make, so it's important to have an understanding of how to weave and loop the thread.

Spaced Intervals

The key to weaving a uniform web is ensuring your anchor points to the hoop are evenly spaced. It can be helpful to think of the hoop as a clock; that is, a circle separated into equal portions. You can use a marker to indicate where to weave the points on the hoop, but make sure you do this on the back of the hoop so the marks can't be seen when your finished dream catcher is on display. The more anchor points you have on the hoop, the more intricate your inner weave will look.

Different Weaves

There are lots of different weaving options for your dream catchers. They all involve looping and knotting threads around a hoop but they give very different weaves. We'll start with simpler weaves and then move on to more complicated designs.

Repetition

Most weaves involve repeating a single step, and in this way they are actually quite easy, despite looking intricate. Once you have the pattern of the weave, you just keep repeating it until you reach the centre of the dream catcher. Simple!

Threading Beads

Beads or charms can be added to your dream-catcher weave at any time. Simply place your chosen bead or charm onto the thread at the desired point. You can make a small knot in the thread on either side of the bead so it doesn't move, but you don't have to.

How Much Thread?

The length of thread you will need for each design will depend on what size hoop you are using. Despite being slightly trickier to work with, it's worth cutting more thread than you think you'll need. But don't worry if you do run out of thread before finishing the inner web; simply tie another length of thread to the end of your first strand and keep going. A useful trick to know how much thread you need for the inner weave is to loosely wrap the thread around the hoop three times and cut it there – that should do it!

Thread Tip

You can wrap your thread around a small piece of cardboard to make weaving easier. Sometimes when weaving thread, it can get tangled; this will prevent that from happening.

Changing Colours

You can change thread colours at different points in your dream-catcher weave. Simply knot the end of your current strand to the new colour thread, add a bead to cover the knot and continue weaving.

Lacy Additions

You can add lace pieces or doilies to your weave to add a bohemian touch. They can be sewn on with thread and form the centrepiece of the dream catcher.

Starry Night

A simple star weave creates a striking dream catcher. This pattern perfectly captures a night star and will ensure your dreams are sweet!

You Will Need:

- One hoop • White cord
- White thread • Craft glue
- Feathers • Scissors

How to Make a Starry-Night Dream Catcher

1. Hold one end of the white cord at the top of the hoop and place some glue under it to secure it to the hoop. Hold the cord end for a minute to let the glue dry.

2. Wrap the cord around the outside of the hoop until you're back where you started. Cut any remaining cord and place some glue under the cord end to secure it in place.

3. Knot the white thread to the top centre of the hoop and trim the end.

4. Bring the thread length to the bottom left of the hoop and loop it around the hoop.

5. Stretch the thread to the top right side of the hoop and loop it.

6. Now stretch the thread to the top left side and loop it.

7. Stretch the thread to the bottom right of the hoop and loop it before returning the thread to the start position at the top centre of the hoop. Tie a knot and trim the end.

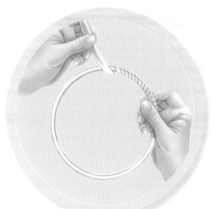

8 Begin the second star by tying the thread to the bottom centre of the hoop, directly opposite the starting point of the first star. Repeat the star pattern.

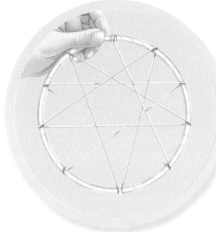

9 Dab some craft glue on each point at the back of the hoop where the thread wraps around. This will keep the thread in place.

10 For the hanging vertical threads, take some white thread and double it over. Place it at the base of the dream catcher and cut it to your desired length.

11 Take the looped end of each thread and place it behind the base of the dream-catcher hoop. Bring the two loose ends up and through the loop to secure the thread to the dream catcher.

12 Tie a feather to the ends of each doubled thread. Repeat for each doubled length of thread.

13 Your starry-night dream catcher is ready to hang (see page 48)!

Coloured Stars

You could use two different-coloured threads in this design, one for each star.

Flower Power

The central weave in this design forms a sweet flower shape. We're going to use multiple thread colours and add some beads and feathers for a decorative twist.

How to Make a Flower-Power Dream Catcher

1 Hold one end of the white cord at the top of the hoop and place some glue under it to secure it to the hoop. Hold the cord end for a minute to let the glue dry.

2 Wrap the cord around the outside of the hoop until you're back where you started. Cut any remaining cord and place some glue under the cord end to secure it in place.

3 Mark seven evenly spaced points on the back of the hoop with the marker.

You Will Need:

- One hoop • White cord
- Green thread • Teal thread
- Light green thread
- Beads • Marker
- Scissors • Ribbons
- Feathers

4 Starting at the point at the top centre of the hoop, knot the green thread to this point and trim the end.

5 Working in a clockwise direction, pull the thread to the next marked point and loop it around the hoop from back to front. Make sure to bring over the previous strand each time, as this will create the loop. Pull the thread.

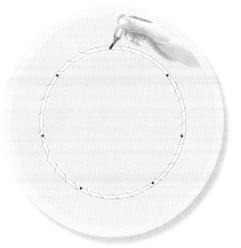

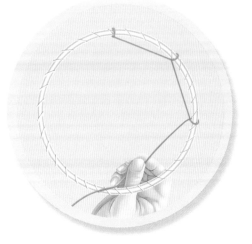

6 Continue until you have looped the thread at all seven points.

7 Once you are back at the beginning, start making the loops onto the centre of each segment, instead of the hoop.

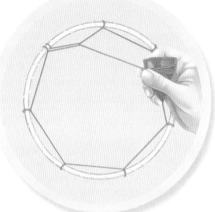

8 Occasionally add a bead onto the thread.

9 Continue this pattern around the hoop one more time with the green thread.

10 Take the teal thread and tie it to the green thread at a point where you're looping a side. This will allow you to hide the knot. Trim the end of the green thread.

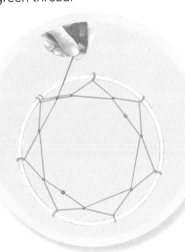

11 Continue the pattern around the circle one more time, looping the thread around the centre of each new segment.

12 Take the light green thread and tie it to the teal thread at a point where you're crossing a side. Trim the end of the teal thread.

13 Continue the pattern, spiralling in towards the middle until you reach the centre.

14 Tie the thread off in the centre of the flower weave and trim the end.

(Continued over)

Flower Power (continued)

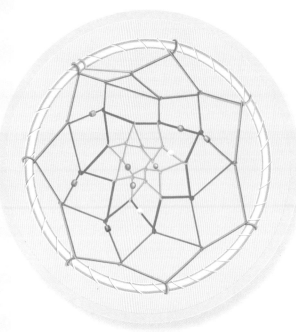

16 Take some green thread and double it over. Place it at the base of the dream catcher and cut it to your desired length.

17 Repeat this three or four times.

18 Take the looped end of each thread and place it behind the base of the hoop. Bring the two loose ends up and through the loop to secure the thread to the hoop.

19 Tie a knot in the doubled thread at any point along the length so you can add a bead. Thread a bead through the thread ends and secure it with another knot. You can add multiple beads to each thread length.

15 It's now time to add your feather and thread embellishments. Choose feathers that match the green tones of the threads and your choice of bead colours.

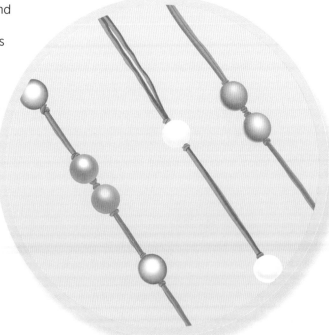

20 Take some teal thread and double it over. Place it at the base of the dream catcher and cut it to your desired length.

21 Repeat this three or four times.

22 Take the looped end of each teal thread and place it behind the base of the hoop. Bring the two loose ends up and through the loop to secure the thread to the hoop. Alternate the green and teal threads.

23 Tie a feather to the end of each doubled thread.

24 Your dream catcher is ready to hang (see page 48)!

Anchoring Embellishments

You can add a dot of craft glue to the hanging feather and bead threads to hold them in place more securely to the thread. You can also add a dot of glue to the rear of each bead. This will be especially important if you plan on hanging your dream catcher outside.

A Spider's Web

Traditionally, dream-catcher weaves were made to resemble spider webs. They often connected to the hoop at eight points, symbolising a spider's eight legs. We're going to replicate this traditional design, but with some modern twists.

You Will Need:

- One hoop
- Black thread • White thread
- Large needle (can be plastic)
- Paper • Pencil
- Marker • Scissors
- Ribbons • Lace ribbon

How to Make a Spider's-Web Dream Catcher

1. Wrap one end of the white thread around the hoop twice and then knot it.

2. Wrap the thread around the hoop until you're back where you started. If any parts of the hoop are showing through the thread, wrap the thread around a second time. Tie the thread to the hoop and cut the ends.

3. Place the piece of paper under the hoop and outline the hoop in pencil. Roughly cut out the paper circle.

4. Fold the circle in half, then in half again and then in half again. The paper is now divided into eight equal sections.

5. Place the paper under the hoop. You need to mark the eight sections. You can do this by marking the eight points with a marker on the back of the hoop.

6   Knot the black thread to the point at the top centre of the hoop.

7   Loop the thread over the hoop and tie a knot at the next marked point at the hoop.

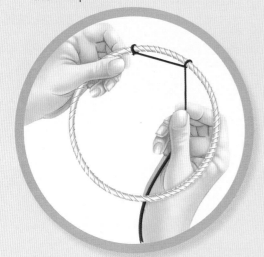

8   Repeat step 7 until you encircle the entire hoop. Refer to the marked dots on the rear of the hoop as you go to ensure your knots are evenly spaced.

9   Place the end of the thread through the needle. A large needle is easiest to work with.

10   Insert the needle under the knot that you made in the first circle and pull the thread through.

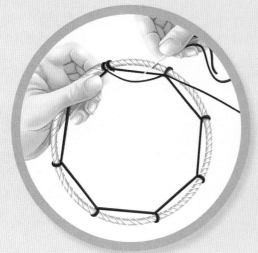

11   Insert the needle into the loop that you just made and pull the thread through. Continue around the circle.

12   As you reach the end of the second circle, you'll see you have made a gap that separates the two parallel loops of thread. This is your first section of spider web.

13   Repeat step 11 two more times.

14   Move on to the next point on the hoop. Insert the needle under the knot and pull the thread through.

15   Insert the needle into the loop that you just made and pull the thread through.

16   As you reach the end of the thread, you'll see you have made a gap that separates the two parallel loops of thread. This is your second section of spider web.

(Continued over)

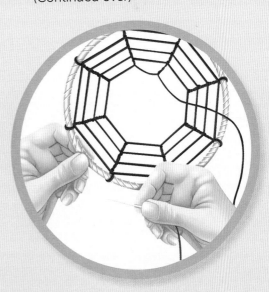

A Spider's Web (continued)

17 Repeat step 15 two more times.

18 Continue this pattern around the hoop, straightening the thread as needed. You may need to pull the web lines towards the centre to make sure they're straight and taut.

19 Once you are back at the start of the hoop, continue the pattern with the row of spider web you just created.

20 Once you reach the centre of the web, the weaving will get quite tight. At this point you can insert the needle through any centre web and tie a knot to secure the thread.

21 Cut any remaining thread. Your spider web weave is now complete!

22 Cut eight lengths of lace ribbon and place them, folded in half, at the base of the dream catcher. Trim them if you'd like them shorter.

23 Take the looped end of each ribbon and place it behind the base of the dream catcher. Bring the two loose ends up and through the loop to secure the ribbon to the dream catcher.

Thread Tip

This design uses a lot more thread than the others in this book. Wrap the black thread around the hoop six times instead of three to figure out how much you need.

24 Your dream catcher is ready to hang (see page 48)!

Crescent Moon

Not all dream catchers have to be made using hoops. You can use sticks from the garden or park — the key is to use ones that don't snap when bent. Greenwood is often best for this; it will dry and turn brown with time.

You Will Need:

- Bendable stick or sticks
- White thread • Scissors
- Beads • Brown cord
- Feathers

How to Make a Crescent-Moon Dream Catcher

1 Find a bendable stick that is curved in the middle. You can also use multiple sticks tied together to form a half circle. If doing this, be sure to tie the sticks together in multiple places so your frame is sturdy.

2 Tie the thread to the top end of the half circle and knot it.

3 Moving from top to bottom, pull the thread from back to front and loop it at evenly spaced intervals. As this is a natural look, the distance between the loops doesn't have to be perfect. Try to have eight or nine points. Make sure to bring over the previous strand each time, as this will create the loop. Pull the thread.

4 Continue until you have looped the thread all the way around the sticks.

5 Once you are at the base of the sticks, flip the dream catcher over and start to make the loops onto the centre of each segment, instead of the sticks.

6 Continue this pattern, always flipping the dream catcher when you reach the end.

7 Occasionally thread a bead onto the thread.

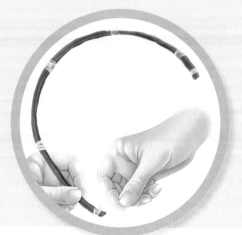

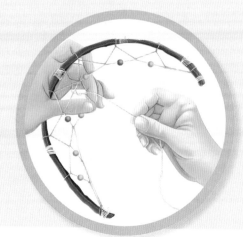

8 Knot the thread at the top or bottom when you have a nice crescent-moon shape.

9 Take several lengths of brown cord and double it over. Place it at the base of the dream catcher and cut it to a short length.

10 Take the looped end of each cord piece and place it behind the dream-catcher frame. Bring the two loose ends up and through the loop to secure the thread to the dream catcher.

11 Tie a feather to each doubled-over cord. Make sure the feathers are quite close to the sticks.

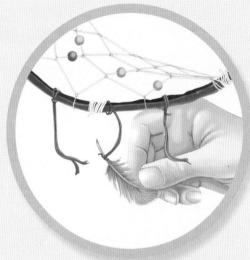

12 Your crescent-moon dream catcher is ready to hang (see page 48)!

Full Moon

Of course, you can use bendable sticks to make a circular dream catcher and weave a full moon. Just be sure to tie the sticks together at multiple points. You can also use other objects, such as an old horseshoe, and weave a simple pattern within it.

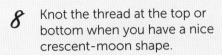

Bright and Happy

Using rainbow thread on a dream catcher makes for a bright and happy look. This design utilises one medium-sized hoop and three smaller ones to create a bold and striking design.

You Will Need:

- One medium hoop
- Three small hoops
- Rainbow-coloured thread
- Marker • Scissors
- Rainbow-coloured ribbon
- Needle • Beads
- Rainbow-coloured feathers

How to Make a Bright-and-Happy Dream Catcher

1. Wrap one end of the rainbow thread around the medium-sized hoop twice and then knot it.

2. Wrap the thread around the hoop until you're back where you started. If any parts of the hoop are showing through the thread, wrap the thread around a second time. Leave the thread attached to the hoop.

3. With the marker, draw eleven evenly spaced marks on the rear of the hoop.

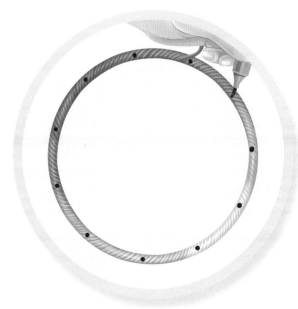

4 Knot the rainbow thread to the point at the top centre of the hoop.

5 Pull the thread to the next marked point and loop around the hoop from back to front. Make sure to bring over the previous strand each time, as this will create the loop. Pull the thread.

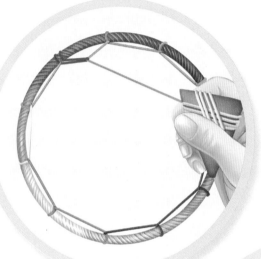

6 Continue until you have looped the thread at all eleven points.

7 Once you are back at the beginning, start to make the loops onto the centre of each segment, instead of the hoop.

8 Thread a bead onto the thread at each loop as you reach the mid-way section of the weave.

9 Continue this pattern around the hoop, spiralling in towards the middle until you reach the centre.

10 Thread a bead into the centre of the weave and tie the thread off in the centre.

11 Take a small hoop and wrap the end of the rainbow thread around it twice and then knot it.

(Continued over)

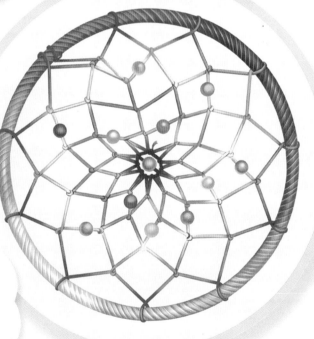

Bead Placement

Beads can be threaded on each loop of the weave or randomly as you go.

Bright and Happy (continued)

12 Wrap the thread around the hoop until you're back where you started. If any parts of the hoop are showing through the thread, wrap the thread around again. Leave the thread attached to the hoop.

13 With the marker, add five evenly spaced marks on the back of the hoop.

14 Starting at the point at the top centre of the hoop, knot the rainbow thread to this point.

15 Pull the thread to the next marked point and loop around the hoop from back to front. Make sure to bring it over the previous strand each time, as this will create the loop. Pull the thread. You may need to thread the needle to do this, as it's easier to use a needle with small hoops.

16 Continue until you have looped the thread at all five points.

17 Once you are back at the beginning, start to make the loops onto the centre of each segment, instead of the hoop.

18 Continue this pattern around the hoop, spiralling in towards the middle until you reach the centre. Tie off the thread in the centre of the weave.

19 Repeat steps 11 to 18 with the other two small hoops.

20 Take small lengths of rainbow thread and tie feathers to them.

21 Tie these threads to the base of the three small hoops.

22 Take the rainbow ribbon and cut three lengths. Place them, folded in half, at the base of the large dream catcher, one towards the left, one in the bottom centre and one towards the right. Ensure they're spaced so that the smaller dream catchers won't touch.

23 Take the looped end of each ribbon and place it behind the dream catcher in the correct position. Bring the two loose ends up and through the loop to secure the ribbon to the dream catcher.

24 Add a bead and tie a small hoop dream catcher to each ribbon.

25 Your dream catcher is ready to hang (see page 48)!

Mix it Up

This design also looks great with one small hoop, if you don't feel like making three.

Make a Rainbow

If you don't have rainbow thread, don't worry – you can make your own. Just wrap the hoops in seven equal sections using thread the colours of the rainbow: red, orange, yellow, green, blue, indigo and violet. You can then use these colours for the central weave, too, by tying a new colour on at regular intervals.

Love Hearts

Dream-catcher frames don't have to be circles — you can use other shapes as your frame. In this design, we'll be using heart shapes. You can buy heart-shaped wire frames at most craft stores.

You Will Need:

- One medium heart-shaped wire frame
- Four small heart-shaped wire frames
- Coloured threads (four colours: we used red, orange, pink and purple)
- White thread • Marker
- Scissors • Needle
- Beads • Feathers

How to Make a Love-Heart Dream Catcher

1   Wrap one end of the coloured thread around the medium-sized heart twice and then knot it.

2   Wrap the thread around one quarter of the heart. Knot the thread and start a new colour. Repeat with the other two colours until the entire heart is covered in four different colours of thread.

3   With the marker, indicate nine spaced marks on the rear of the heart.

4 Starting at any point at the top of the hoop, knot the white thread to this point.

8 Continue the pattern, spiralling in towards the middle of the heart until you reach the centre. The weave won't be perfectly symmetrical because of the heart shape.

5 Pull the thread to the next marked point and loop around the heart from back to front. Make sure to bring it over the previous strand each time, as this will create the loop. Pull the thread.

6 Continue until you have looped the thread at all nine points.

7 Once you are back at the beginning, start to make the loops onto the centre of each segment, instead of the heart.

9 Tie the thread off in the centre of the weave.

10 Take a small heart and wrap a coloured-thread end around it twice and then knot it.

11 Wrap the thread around the frame until you're a quarter of the way around the heart. Knot the thread and start a new colour. Repeat with two more colours until the entire heart is covered in thread.

12 With the marker, indicate five evenly spaced marks on the rear of the heart.

13 Starting at the point at the top centre of the heart, knot the white thread to this point.

(Continued over)

Love Hearts (continued)

14 Pull the thread to the next marked point and loop around the heart from back to front. Make sure to bring it over the previous strand each time, as this will create the loop. Pull the thread. You may need to thread the needle to do this as it's easier to use a needle with small frames.

15 Continue until you have looped the thread at all five points.

16 Once you are back at the beginning, start to make the loops onto the centre of each segment, instead of the heart.

17 Continue this pattern around the heart, spiralling in towards the middle until you reach the centre. Tie off the thread in the centre of the weave.

18 Repeat steps 10 to 17 with the other three small hearts.

19 Loop a length of thread at the base of the medium heart. Thread a bead through the thread ends and tie one of the small hearts to the thread.

20 Do this again at the base of the small heart you just tied, so two small hearts dangle from the base of the larger heart.

21 Attach the other two small hearts to either side of the larger heart in the same way, threading beads on these as well.

22 Tie feathers and beads to short lengths of thread and attach several to each of the love hearts.

23 Your dream catcher is ready to hang (see page 48)!

Heart in Heart

For a different look, you could add a cardboard heart cut-out to the inside of the larger heart and not include a weave at all.

Owl

Combining a dream-catcher design with a bird really makes the most of the feathers used in dream catchers. This striking design looks great and is more of a decorative piece than the other dream catchers we've created so far.

How to Make an Owl Dream Catcher

1 Hold the light blue cord end at the top of one of the hoops and place some glue under it to secure it to the hoop. Hold the cord end for a minute to let the glue dry.

2 Wrap the cord around the outside of the hoop until you're back where you started. Leave a length of cord hanging at the top of the hoop.

3 Repeat steps 1 and 2 with the other small hoop.

You Will Need:

- Two small hoops • Light blue cord
- White thread • Needle • Marker
- Scissors • 2 large wooden beads
- 3 medium wooden beads
- Additional beads (optional)
- Feathers, large and small • Craft glue

4 At this point, it is a good idea to lay the hoops next to each other and place the feathers and beads around them. This will help you get the look and feel of your owl before committing to your design. You can make changes as you wish until you're happy with your owl.

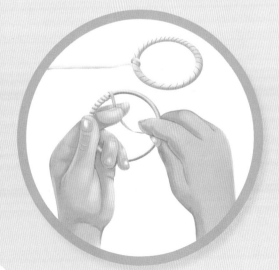

5 With the marker, add eight evenly spaced marks on the back of one of the hoops.

9 Once you are back at the beginning, start to make the loops on the centre of each segment instead of the hoop.

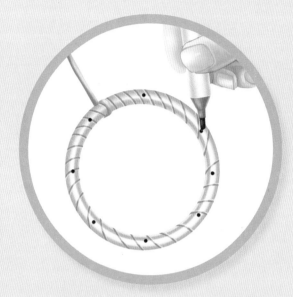

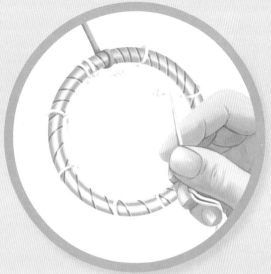

6 Starting at the point at the top centre of the hoop, knot the white thread to this point.

7 Pull the thread to the next marked point and loop around the hoop from back to front. Make sure to bring it over the previous strand each time as this will create the loop. Pull the thread. You may need to thread the needle to do this, as it's easier to use a needle with small hoops.

8 Continue until you have looped the thread at all eight points.

10 Continue this pattern around the hoop, spiralling inwards until you reach the centre. Thread on the bead you have chosen for the owl's eye. Tie the thread off in a knot.

(Continued over)

Owl (continued)

11 Repeat steps 5 to 10 with the other small hoop.

12 Making sure the hanging cords are at the tops of the hoops, take a small length of white thread and tie the two hoops together so they form a figure of eight. Wrap the thread around the middle a few times to secure the hoops together securely. Tie a knot and trim the end.

13 To make the hanging section, take the two cords left hanging at the top of the hoops and tie them together. Trim any excess.

14 Cut 10 lengths of light blue thread or cord (cord does work better). Fold them in half, then take the looped ends of each thread and place them behind the base of the dream catcher. Bring the two loose ends up and through the loop to secure the thread to the dream catcher. Do this for each of the lengths of thread, five on each hoop.

Hiding Knots

Knots can be hidden by placing them at the back of the hoop. Twist the knot until it can no longer be seen from the front of the dream catcher.

15 To make the beak, thread a bead through the strand of thread closest to the meeting point of both hoops on the left hoop. Thread another bead through the strand of thread closest to the meeting point on the right hoop. Now thread a bead through both strings. These three beads will form a triangular beak shape. Tie a knot to secure them.

16 Tie the feathers on. Try to form a bird shape.

17 Glue some feathers to the back of the cord at the top of each hoop to give the owl eyebrows.

18 Your owl dream catcher is ready to hang!

Shapes

As we hope this design shows you, dream catchers can be made into many different things. Don't feel limited by shapes. Have a good look at your craft or fabric store to find other shapes you could use.

Double Hoop

A modern dream-catcher design twist is to use a smaller hoop within a larger hoop. Weaving the smaller hoop to the larger hoop forms the inner woven section. Leaving the smaller hoop unwoven allows the wall colour to show through.

You Will Need:

- One large hoop
- One small hoop
- White thread
- Bright pink thread
- Coloured threads (seven different colours)
- Scissors • Beads
- Paper • Craft glue
- Feathers

How to Make a Double-Hoop Dream Catcher

1. Wrap one end of the white thread around the small hoop twice and then knot it.

2. Wrap the thread around the hoop until you're back where you started. Be sure to wrap the knot so it can't be seen. If any parts of the hoop are showing through the thread, wrap the thread around again. Tie the thread to the hoop and keep the thread attached, as we'll use it later.

3. Wrap another piece of white thread around the large hoop twice and then knot it.

4. Wrap the thread around the hoop. Change to pink thread once you've covered a third of the hoop by knotting some pink thread on and continuing to wrap until the hoop is covered.

5 Place the smaller hoop inside the larger hoop and position it towards the bottom right.

6 Take the piece of white thread attached to the small hoop and wrap it around the top of the large hoop. Wrap the thread back around the small hoop. Do this a few times and then tie it to the large hoop. Trim the end.

7 Take a length of pink thread and tie it to the large hoop. Loop the thread through the large and small hoops.

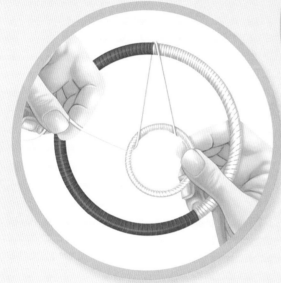

8 Go around the hoops a couple of times until you are happy with the amount of thread.

9 Tie the pink thread to the large hoop and trim the end.

(Continued over)

Top Tip

The inner frame you use for this design does not have to be round. You could use a square or heart-shaped frame instead.

Double Hoop (continued)

10 For this modern look, we are going to add a lot of threads to hang from the base of the dream catcher. Cut several long lengths of each of the seven thread colours. Fold them all in half.

11 Place all the folded threads at the base of the dream catcher. Separate them by colour (you can repeat colours). Take the looped end of each colour thread and bring the loose ends up and through the loop.

14 Comb the fringe with your fingers so the threads are as straight as possible. Place the triangle on top of the fringe.

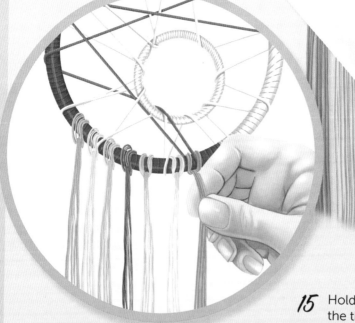

12 Run your hands through the threads so they don't tangle.

13 For even more of a modern touch, we're going to trim the threads into a point. To do this, cut a large triangle from the paper.

15 Hold the paper down and trim along the thread edges with the scissors to form a triangle.

16 Take the feathers and beads and tie them to the thread ends. You could add a dot of glue if needed.

17 Your double-hoop dream catcher is ready to hang (see page 48)!

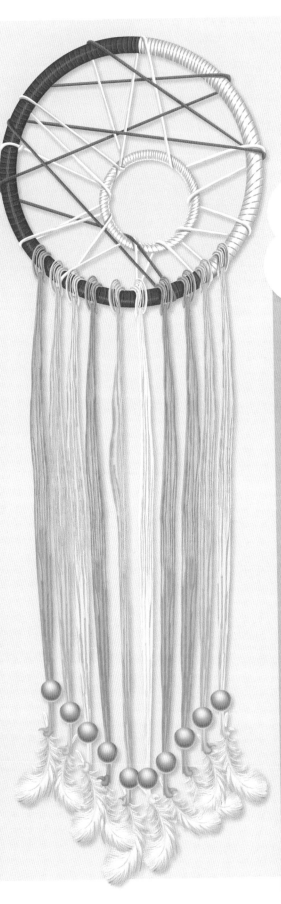

Huge Hoops

You can make very large dream catchers using large hoops. You could even make one on a hula hoop! When working on such a large-scale design, wool should be used for the inner weave.

Necklace

Not all dream catchers need to hang above your bed – you can make wearable dream catchers! This simple necklace will display your dream-catcher skills in a completely new way.

How to Make a Necklace Dream Catcher

1   Wrap one end of the red thread around the small hoop twice and then knot it.

2   Wrap the thread around the hoop until you're back where you started. Be sure to wrap the knot so it can't be seen. If any parts of the hoop are showing through the thread, wrap the thread around a second time. Tie off the thread with a knot.

3   With the marker, indicate eight evenly spaced marks on the rear of the hoop.

You Will Need:

- One very small hoop
- Red thread • Blue thread
- Black cord • Scissors
- Needle • Beads
- Craft glue
- Marker

4   Starting at the point at the top centre of the hoop, knot the blue thread to this point.

5   Pull the thread to the next marked point and loop around the hoop from back to front. Make sure to bring over the previous strand each time, as this will create the loop. Pull the thread. You may need to thread the needle to do this, as it's easier to use a needle with small hoops.

6   Continue until you have looped the thread at all eight points.

7   Once you are back at the beginning, start to make the loops onto the centre of each segment instead of the hoop.

8   Continue this pattern around the hoop, spiralling in towards the middle until you reach the centre. Thread a bead into the central section. Tie the thread off in a knot.

9   Cut a piece of cord the length that you want the necklace. Tie a double-knot at the end. Loop one end of the thread through the top of the dream catcher. Pass the knot through the open circle of the cord and pull tightly to secure it.

10 Cut three short lengths of blue thread and tie a knot at the bottom of each. Thread some small beads onto each thread. Glue these threads to the rear of the hoop.

11 Your dream-catcher necklace is ready to wear!

Plastic Bracelet

You could use a plastic bracelet as the hoop to make this necklace!

Hanging Your Dream Catcher

There are lots of different ways you can hang your dream catchers. We'll show you a simple way that looks great with any dream catcher.

How to Hang Your Dream Catcher

1. Cut a length of thread or cord about 26 centimetres (10 inches) long.

2. Fold it in half and tie a knot in the end.

3. Thread a bead or two through the looped end. This step is optional.

4. Wrap the looped end underneath the back of the dream catcher at the top.

5. Bring the knotted end and bead through the loop and pull tight.

6. Your hanging loop is complete and you can hang your dream catcher!

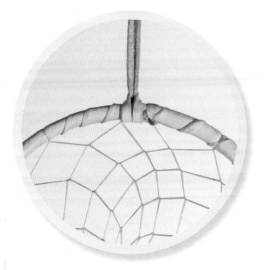

Dream Catcher Mobile

You can also hang your dream catcher as a mobile. It will need to be secured from the ceiling and, depending on the size of the hoop, might need three to five hanging loops to hold it horizontally instead of vertically.